T0132213

Mala Discovers

by Alexandria Pereira

AuthorHouse™
1663 Liberty Drive
Bloomington, IN 47403
www.authorhouse.com
Phone: 833-262-8899

Because of the dynamic nature of the Internet, any web addresses or links contained in this book may have changed since publication and may no longer be valid. The views expressed in this work are solely those of the author and do not necessarily reflect the views of the publisher, and the publisher hereby disclaims any responsibility for them.

This book is printed on acid-free paper.

ISBN: 979-8-8230-1568-4 (sc)
ISBN: 979-8-8230-1580-6 (hc)
ISBN: 979-8-8230-1569-1 (e)

Library of Congress Control Number: 2023919166

Print information available on the last page.

Published by AuthorHouse 10/18/2023

authorHOUSE®

The Mystery of History Series
India
Book 2 of 4

To my grandma, whose life work was dedicated to
children and their pursuit of knowledge.

"Grandma, where do I come from?" asked Mala.

"I am so glad you asked, Mala. I was just looking at pictures of our family. Here is a picture of your mother, who is my child. And this is your great-grandmother, who is my mother. She had a mother too. We are all part of a family that started a long, long time ago," replied Grandma.

"Where did they all come from?" asked Mala.

"Would you like to go to the history museum today and find out?" asked Grandma.

"Yes, it's a mystery to me," replied Mala.

"History is what happened a week ago, a month ago, and so many years ago. History is a lot of fun because it tells the story of how people lived and learned new things. We call every person who lived before us our ancestor. Our ancestors added to who we are, what we know, and what we can do.

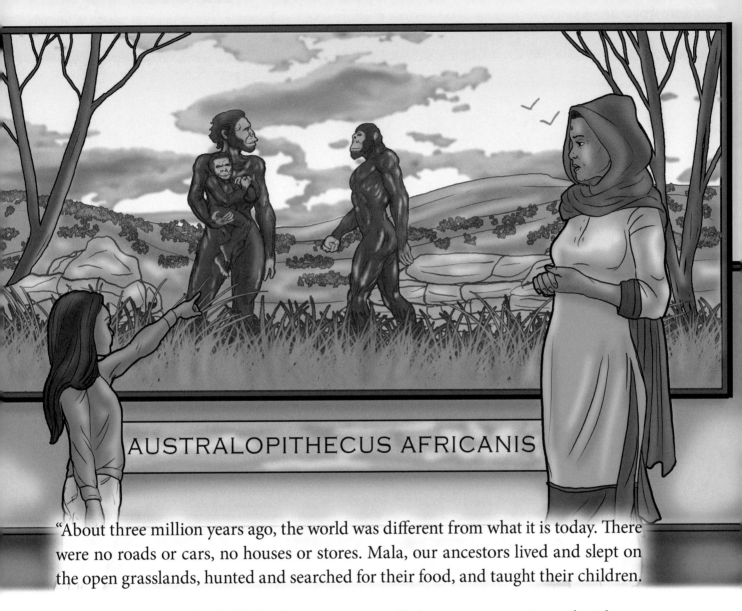

AUSTRALOPITHECUS AFRICANIS

"About three million years ago, the world was different from what it is today. There were no roads or cars, no houses or stores. Mala, our ancestors lived and slept on the open grasslands, hunted and searched for their food, and taught their children.

Our first ancestors looked like this. Scientists call these ancestors *Australopithecus afarensis*. They lived on the continent of Africa," said Grandma.
"But we live in India, Grandma," said Mala.
"Yes, we do live in India, but our ancestors first lived in Africa," replied Grandma.
"Grandma, did I come from her?" asked Mala.
"Yes, Mala, she is our ancestor," replied Grandma.

"About 1.8 million years ago, our ancestors grew to look like this. Scientist call them *Homo erectus*. They walked out of Africa and walked all the way to India looking for food.

Then about one hundred thousand years later, more of our ancestors, called *Homo sapiens*, walked out of Africa and into India, following the animals they were hunting," said Grandma.

"That is a long way to walk," said Mala.

"Yes, it is," said Grandma.

"Then seventy-five thousand years ago, the largest volcano ever, the Mount Toba volcano in Sumatra, Indonesia, erupted. The ash from the volcano filled the sky and blocked the sun, which caused an ice age. For more than twenty-five thousand years, no new ancestors walked from Africa to India, because the ground, in between, was covered with ice and snow," said Grandma.

"Look Grandma, the volcano is erupting," exclaimed Mala.

"After the ice age ended, more ancestors, called the Denisovans, came to India. There they met our other ancestors and had children together. These children grew and had children of their own. They worked hard, worked together, and learned new things. They lived on the open plains of India in small families. They hunted and gathered for their food and learned how to make a very important thing—fire. With fire, people could cook their food, keep warm, and defend themselves," said Grandma.

"What kinds of food did they cook?" asked Mala.

"Mostly different kinds of meat," replied Grandma.

"Next our ancestors started living in caves to keep warm and dry. They carved and painted maps of the stars in the sky, pretty designs, and animals such as ostriches and giraffes on the walls of the caves. They told stories about their history to their friends and family.

"These ancestors then became what we call the Adivasi people. They lived and traveled in the forested part of India in tribes. They hunted, gathered, and started to farm for their food.

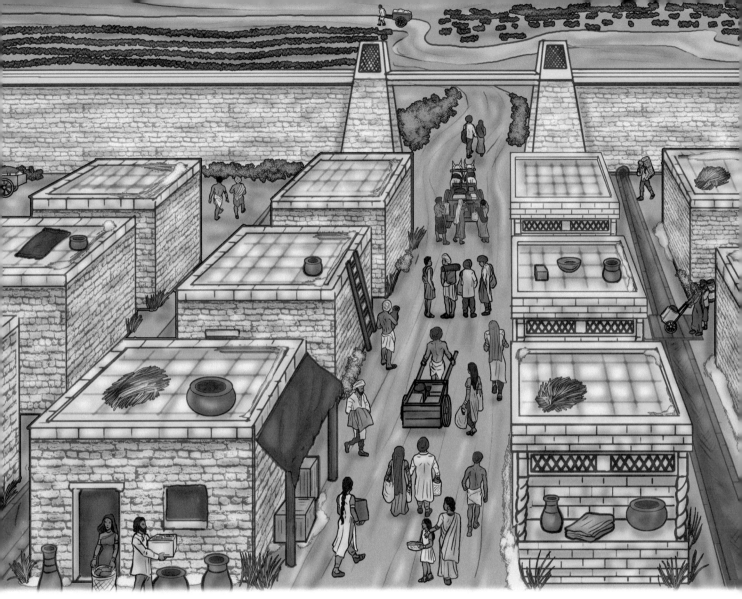

"Next more ancestors came to India. They started building houses and farms. They lived in an area we call Mehrgarh. Then, for some reason, all the people left Mehrgarh," said Grandma.

"Why did they leave?" asked Mala.

"We do not know why. But they left their houses and farms and never returned. Mehrgarh was forgotten.

"The people from Mehrgarh walked east, building new houses, buildings, and farms along the Indus River Valley. We call this new area Harappan. Did you know that India was named after the Indus River?" asked Grandma.

"No, I did not," replied Mala.

"The Harappan people worked hard and worked together. They grew food to eat such as peas, wheat, mangos, melons, and dates. They herded their cattle, water buffalo, sheep, and goats in pens and on the open grasslands near their towns.

"The Harappan people grew more food, like barley and lentils and made pottery, which they traded with people far away for jewels and different kinds of wood. Then they used those things to make bracelets, beads, and small animal figures," said Grandma.

"Like these?" asked Mala.

"Yes, like those. They would trade those things for other things they needed and built more houses, bigger buildings, and more farms. This trading made a lot of money, and they built docks on the rivers for boats and carts pulled by bullocks to carry things they were trading.

"The Harappan people built their houses with strong bricks that were all the same size. They built strong walls around their towns. They made wells to get fresh water. They built cooking ovens like the tandoors we still use today. And they had writing. This was stamped on many buildings. But no one can read this writing today because the language of the Harappans has been lost. Can you guess what this says?" asked Grandma.

"Well, maybe something about wheels, carts and tools," replied Mala.

"You could be right. Maybe one day we will know.

"Then for some reason—we don't know exactly why—the Harappan people stopped trading, farming, and making bricks and left their cities. Over time sand covered their homes and buildings, and the Harappan cities were lost and forgotten. The people of Harappan might have moved to southern India, but we do not know for sure.

"Then came people called the Aryans. They brought horses, ways to work with metal, and the Sanskrit language to India. They lived in small huts in small villages. They ate wheat and rice and drank milk. They worked hard to keep themselves safe. They built the first universities and wrote some of the earliest stories, called the Vedas, about how people came to live in India.

"With all these people now in India, there were many small kingdoms. The people continued to work hard to find and grow food, stay dry and warm, and keep themselves safe. But they fought each other for power.

This allowed a Greek man, named Alexander the Great, to march his armies all the way to India and take over some of those kingdoms. But Alexander's soldiers had been marching for eight whole years, and they were tired when they reached India. They wanted to go home, and they did.

"As Alexander the Great's soldiers were leaving, a king from southern India took control of these kingdoms. His name was Chandragupta Maurya. He helped the people be stronger and build better houses, and he helped make trading easier. Then his grandson, Ashoka, became king. Ashoka took control of almost all the rest of India.

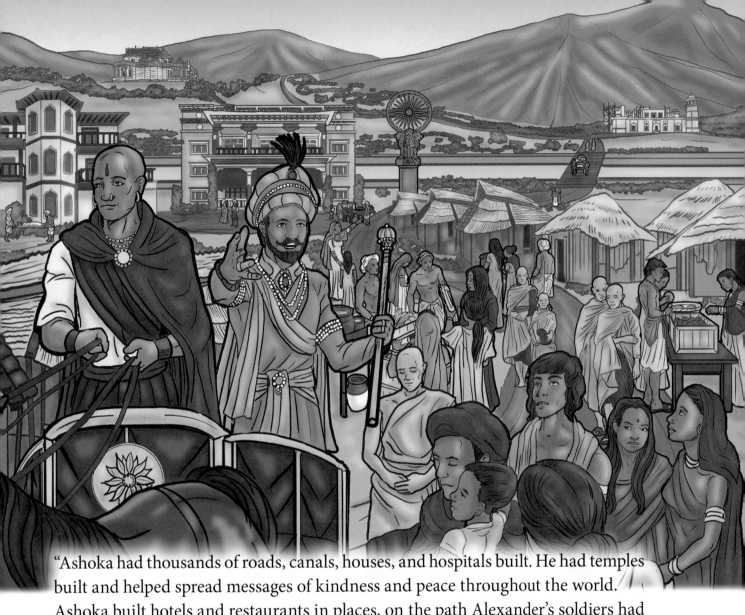

"Ashoka had thousands of roads, canals, houses, and hospitals built. He had temples built and helped spread messages of kindness and peace throughout the world. Ashoka built hotels and restaurants in places, on the path Alexander's soldiers had traveled on, so that traders would have a place to eat and sleep as they traveled. We call this path, the Silk Road," said Grandma.

"Do you know what this is?" asked Grandma.

"Yes, it is the Ashoka Chakra, on the flag of India," replied Mala.

"Yes, and it tells how to live your life in peace," said Grandma.

"Next came the Gupta Empire. Its people had enough food, felt safe, and wrote stories about the history of India.

Then more armies came, including the Huns. India went back to being many kingdoms again, with all of them fighting one another for power.
It took the people of India another five hundred years to find ways to work together again," said Grandma.

"Grandma, I have learned a lot today about our ancestors—the Adivasi, Mehrgarh, Harappan, and Aryans. I learned how all my ancestors had ancestors who walked out of Africa. I learned how hard they all worked, helping their families find food, stay safe and dry, and grow so that I could be here today, learning about where I come from. Thank you, Grandma," said Mala.

"You are welcome, Mala," said Grandma.

Timeline of Indian History

3 million BC	The first human ancestors, the *Australopithecus afarensis*, appear in the Cradle of Humankind, situated in today's South Africa.
1.8 million	Early *Homo erectus* appear on the continent of Africa, and some start walking to India.
300,000	Early *Homo sapiens* appear on the southern shores of South Africa, and start walking to India.
50,000	Denisovans appear on the Indian subcontinent.
9,000	Rock shelters are painted with figures of animals and celestial scenes. At the same time, the Nishadas and Kiratas tribes come to the Indian subcontinent.
7000	The Mehrgarh culture thrives.
3300 to 1300	The Harappan civilization thrives.
1500	The Aryan people from Kazakhstan settle on northern Indian subcontinent.
1500	The first of four Vedic texts were composed.
322	The Maurya Empire starts.
327	Alexander the Great conquers India's northeastern kingdoms to Indus River.
300	The Silk Road starts to be very active in trading goods.
329	The kingdom of Magadha and Maurya Empire take back the northeastern kingdoms.
265–238	The reign of Ashoka, a brutal ruler turned devout follower of Buddhism.
130	The Silk Road expands to include trade between China and the West.
AD 320–550	The Gupta Empire thrives and fosters many discoveries in math, astronomy, and writing, including the Gita.
430	The Huns attack, and northern India breaks up again into warring kingdoms.

Educational Support Activities

Basic Human Needs

We need food to eat, clothing to keep us warm, and shelter to keep us safe and dry.
We need to socialize to work together.
We need to solve problems so that we can invent and be creative.

Practical Life and Sensorial Foundation

Plant a seed. Cook some rice. Hang clothes on a clothesline. Why do we do these things?

History

Make stamps out of dough. Use those stamps to make a message, like the Harappans did many years ago, or stamp them on a timeline.
Dough:
Mix and knead together 2 cups of salt, 5 cups of flour, and 2 cups of warm water until smooth. Roll it out to 2½ inches thick. Cut seals out, and either carve in or put more dough on to make designs. Bake at 150 degrees Celsius until the seals are dry all the way through. Cool and then paint, glaze, and use with ink.

Language

Write your name in Sanskrit.
Mala = मल
Grandma = मातामही

Geography and Map Work

Find the Harrapan River Valley on a map, and trace it with your finger. Who are its neighbors?

Science

Model the Harrapan River Valley in dirt. Pour water, and watch it flow to the ocean.

Botany

What foods are gown in India? Eat some rice, wheat, and red lentils.

Printed in the United States
by Baker & Taylor Publisher Services